A SEAGULL IN THE HAMPTONS

a comedy in four acts
freely adapted from
Anton Chekhov's
THE SEAGULL
by

Emily Mann

BROADWAY PLAY PUBLISHING INC
224 E 62nd St, NY, NY 10065
www.broadwayplaypub.com
info@broadwayplaypub.com

Cover poster design by Cynthia Boone

I S B N: 978-0-88145-561-8

First printing: May 2013
Second printing: November 2015

Book design: Marie Donovan
Page make-up: Adobe Indesign
Typeface: Palatino
Printed and bound in the U S A

A SEAGULL IN THE HAMPTONS received its world premiere in May 2008 at the McCarter Theatre Center (Emily Mann, Artistic Director/Resident Playwright; Jeffrey Woodward, Managing Director) in Princeton, NJ. The cast and creative contributors were as follows:

MARIA...Maria Tucci
NICHOLAS..Brian Murray
ALEX ....Stark Sands
NINA...Morena Baccarin
PHILIP ....David Andrew Macdonald
BEN ....Larry Pine
LORENZO ....Daniel Oreskes
PAULA... Jacqueline Antaramian
MILLY..Laura Heisler
HAROLD.. Matthew Maher

Director ....Emily Mann
Set design .... Eugene Lee
Costume design ....Jennifer von Mayrhauser
Lighting design ....Jane Cox
Original music ....Baikida Carroll
Sound design ....Karin Graybash
Dramaturgy ....Carrie Hughes
Production stage manager .... Cheryl Mintz

CHARACTERS

MARIA, *an actress*
NICHOLAS, *her brother*
ALEX, *her son*
NINA, *the daughter of a neighbor*
PHILIP, *a writer*
BEN, *a doctor*
LORENZO, *the caretaker and cook*
PAULA, *his wife*
MILLY, *their daughter*
HAROLD, *a school teacher*

for Gary

ACT ONE

(MARIA *and* NICHOLAS'*s house in Quogue, New York. A make-shift theater on the beach. Chairs)*

(HAROLD *and* MILLY:)

HAROLD: Maybe black just isn't your color.

MILLY: What? What are you talking about?

HAROLD: Well...why do you *always* wear black? It's summer for Chrissake!

MILLY: I'm in mourning...for my life. I'm unhappy, Harold.

HAROLD: Oh, come *on*! *You're* unhappy? Why? You live on a gorgeous estate! On the beach! Your parents make a great living working here! You—

MILLY: Will you stop? It's not *about* money! With you, everything's always about money. What's wrong with you?

HAROLD: Well, as they say, rich or poor it's good to have money!

MILLY: I never thought that joke was funny.

HAROLD: Look—do you hear me complaining? I live with my...crazy mother, two bratty sisters and my pathetic little brother in a three bedroom walk-up in town...

MILLY: I know that, Harold.

HAROLD: I made $21,550 last year *before taxes.* My mother won't work; we can't afford health insurance; my sister needs—

MILLY: When is the play going to start?

HAROLD: I don't know. Oh, God… can you imagine what it must feel like to be them? He writes a play —she stars in it—they both get swept away by each other's genius. I mean, really… Some people are just born with it all—looks, talent, money…PLUS they're madly in love with each other.

MILLY: Don't make me sick.

HAROLD: I know. Who wants to marry a man who can't afford his own funeral?

MILLY: Look!—Harold! I'm well…touched by your affection; I just can't return it, okay? *(Pause)* Cigarette?

HAROLD: No, thanks.

MILLY: You know…I would gladly be homeless? Begging on the street…if I was—if only I was…well… if only the right person would just—oh, God, never mind. You could never understand.

(Enter ALEX *And his uncle,* NICHOLAS, *conversing.)*

ALEX: You should live in the City, Uncle Nick, and stop complaining about the country all the time.

NICHOLAS: I know!

ALEX: *(Seeing* MILLY *and* HAROLD*)* What are you two doing here? I told you I'd call you when the play was going to start.

MILLY: Okay.

NICHOLAS: *(To* MILLY:*)* Milly, I really wish you'd tell your father to do something about that dog. His barking keeps me up at night.

MILLY: I don't speak to my father. I can't stand him. So don't ask me. *(To* HAROLD*)* Come on, Harold.

HAROLD: Don't forget to let us know when the play starts!

*(*HAROLD *and* MILLY *exit.)*

NICHOLAS: Look at me! Dressed to the nines and nowhere to go!

ALEX: Get a grip, Uncle Nick.

*(*NICHOLAS *shoves on his sunglasses.)*

NICHOLAS: I finally got to sleep last night and woke up at ten-thirty this morning feeling like my brains were stuck to my skull. I thought sea air was supposed to be good for you, but my bowels are made of cement, I have this raging head-ache, and Goddammit! That dog is going to howl all night again tonight, and tomorrow night, and the night after that—and I won't get a wink of sleep—ever! …These people drive me crazy. Why do I come out here? Why do I even bother trying to have a nice time? Every year it's the same thing. I arrive and before the end of the first day—the very first day—I wish I'd never come! And for some incomprehensible reason, I have decided to retire out here! Can you believe it? What could have possessed me to do that? Retirement's a mug's game, Alex. Old people should never have been born.

ALEX: Uh… Okay… What do you think of my stage? It's Peter Brook's empty space.

NICHOLAS: Who?

ALEX: No scenery, no props, no lights—just the ocean, the horizon and a curtain. The play starts at exactly eight-thirty when the moon rises.

NICHOLAS: Brilliant.

ALEX: Well,… that is, if Nina isn't late. If she is, the whole thing will be a fiasco. The play is dependent on being completely in synch with nature. Oh, God! She should have been here by now! Her parents are like complete and total *jailers*! They don't want her coming over here so she has to sneak out of the house to do it. They think we're a terrible influence— show business people and … degenerate…liberals… Actually, you know, you kind of could use a shave, Uncle Nick. Her parents probably see you and worry that… Oh, I don't know.

NICHOLAS: You're right. And I always wonder why women never find me attractive. If I'd only shave!

ALEX: No, I didn't mean…

NICHOLAS: Why is your mother being so impossible? Do you know? She's incredibly cranky and bitchy … I hate it when she's like this.

ALEX: She's bored out of her mind out here! And she's probably insanely jealous of Nina because Nina's acting in my play, and she isn't. She can't bear that tonight won't be all about *her*, and I also bet she's afraid her stupid boyfriend will fall all over himself when he sees Nina. I mean, what man wouldn't? Nina's gorgeous, and young and talented. My mother's pathetic and old, and she won't admit it, and she can't stand it. Her glory days are over, so even though she hasn't seen my play yet, she already decided she hates it.

NICHOLAS: Oh, stop it.

ALEX: Why? You know I'm right. You can't mention another actresses' name in her presence without her going crazy. You can't talk about anyone in the theater but her. Mention Meryl Streep and she has a stroke. She has to be the complete center of attention and as soon as she isn't, she wants to leave, or change the

subject back to her! And have you noticed that she
is completely and totally...stingy? I mean, I asked to
borrow some money last month—I mean, to take Nina
out to dinner, like fifty bucks or something. I didn't
want to put a down-payment on a house or anything!
—and she started to have an asthma attack! I mean,
I know for a fact she has a ton of money in the bank
and—

NICHOLAS: Relax. You're just nervous about your play.
Your mother adores you.

ALEX: My mother hates me. I'm nineteen years old and
a constant reminder to her that she's not thirty-two.
Her whole life is the 'theatuh'! And she knows I hate
the theater.

NICHOLAS: What do you mean? You've just written a
play!

ALEX: No, no! Not pure theater. I don't hate that. I
hate her kind of theater! It's so fake! People marching
around pretending like they're in some living room.
I mean, all they do is talk and they're boring and
pathetic and old...and they have nothing to say. I
mean, who cares, really? The world is falling apart, or
worse, the planet is dying! And these people go to the
theatre to be entertained by people who are just like
them—or even worse, more clueless than they are!
And because the producers are so concerned about not
offending anybody while they pay their 100 fucking
dollars, there is nothing controversial or worthwhile
going on. Unless, of course it's from England! Then
of course like good colonialists we bow down to their
British accents—anything in British accents makes
Americans feel inferior, especially in the theater— and
we say it's brilliant, even when it's just—pretentious
crap or little dramas with tiny little morals posing as
great art—or those fucking cheerful musicals! Oh my

God! I don't know. The whole New York theatre scene makes me sick.

NICHOLAS: Well, I can't blame you.

ALEX: We have to have a new kind of theater, that's all. Something vibrant, and young, and dangerous and alive or, you know what? Just have nothing at all!

NICHOLAS: We have to have theater, Alex.

ALEX: No, we don't! *Why do we have to have theater*? I mean, I love my mother but she leads such a stupid life! She dedicates every waking hour to something that just doesn't matter! And you can imagine how utterly revolting it feels to be me! Here I am at all her stupid parties full of celebrities and people who have all won prizes for something or other—you know, it's ridiculous! Pulitzers and Nobels, and book awards, and Oscars and Tonys and all that crap and here I am! I have nothing to say for myself; I can't even understand what they're talking about half the time; and they're all wondering how Maria could have spawned such a pathetic little loser.

NICHOLAS: That's absolutely not true. You are a talented, good-looking, adorable young man… What I *don't* understand about your mother is this boyfriend of hers. What sort of guy is he? I know he's a famous writer, but he's too young for her, and I know for a fact he's running around with every available woman in New York! The technically unavailable ones, too. Doesn't she have any pride?

ALEX: Oh, Philip's alright. I mean, his writing is nothing much, but he's the best she can do. I mean, just look at her! Why can't she act middle-aged like everybody else's mother?

NICHOLAS: Well, I can't really blame her for living with Philip. I love being around literary people, too.

I always wanted to be a writer, you know, and I guess I'm not... There's a great New Yorker cartoon. I wonder if you've seen it...? Two people are at a party and a middle-aged guy is holding his drink, talking to this beautiful woman and the guy says "Well, I'm a writer. Of course, I haven't actually written anything yet." Oh, God. *(Laughing)* That absolutely cracks me up...

ALEX: I don't get it...

NICHOLAS: You see, Alex, when I was your age, I only really wanted two things in life—one: to be a writer, and two: to have a passionate love affair with a gorgeous, talented woman, marry her and be hopelessly in love with my wife for the rest of my life. Unfortunately, I didn't do that either... Take heed, my friend...I've ended up a boring, old, retired lawyer— with nothing to do...and no one to love.... It's actually pretty funny when you think about it—

ALEX: It is?

(NINA enters breathless.)

ALEX: Nina! Nina, Nina, Nina, Nina, Nina....

NINA: I'm not late, am I? I ran all the way over.

(ALEX and NINA start kissing madly.)

ALEX: NO, NO... *(Kissing)* No, you're fine, it's fine...

(Kissing)

NINA: *(Seeing NICHOLAS)* Oh, hello... They wouldn't let me out all day!

NICHOLAS: You're crying!

NINA: Oh, no. I'm just so glad to be here. *(To ALEX)* My father doesn't know I'm here. I'll have to run back right after.

ALEX: Oh, no! Don't do that. You can't! Oh, God. It's time to start. I'll go get everybody.

NICHOLAS: No, no, no. I'll go. *(He goes.)*

NINA: My parents don't want me here. They're so afraid I'll become an actress! Oh, God, I love you so much!

(ALEX and NINA kiss.)

ALEX: Oh, Nina, you have no idea how much I—

(ALEX and NINA kiss.)

ALEX: The moon's coming up. Just like we planned.

NINA: Yes. Oh, Alex, I hope I'm alright. Your play is so hard to act. It's hard to play someone who isn't alive.

ALEX: But you're wonderful and living people on stage…well, that's over.

NINA: I know.

(ALEX and NINA kiss.)

ALEX: We have to go.

(As ALEX and NINA exit behind the stage:)

ALEX: Remember, be ready for the stink bomb!

(BEN and PAULA enter.)

PAULA: Oh, God, it's so damp tonight. You should go back and put on some long pants, some warm socks, or…some rubbers.

BEN: Rubbers?! What are you? Something out of the nineteenth century?

PAULA: You're wearing tennis shoes with holes and your feet will get wet, and you're always catching cold! You're the doctor! Why do I have to be telling you this? You don't take care of yourself.

BEN: I'm fine! In fact, I'm hot.

PAULA: You spent the night with her out in the garden, didn't you?

BEN: What?

PAULA: Listen, just admit it. You're in love with Maria! I mean, I know you are. Everyone is.

BEN: What do you want from me?

PAULA: It's just sickening. All of you—you see an actress, and you just fall at her feet!

BEN: Oh, Paula, knock it off.

PAULA: Women are always falling in love with you, so I—I—

BEN: Of course woman fall in love with me—I deliver their babies! That's all there is to it. Then they go home to their nice husbands with their nice babies and I don't see them again until they come in for their check-ups once a year. For Christ's sake, I am an honorable man, Paula, and a first-rate doctor, and I don't appreciate—

PAULA: I know you are. Oh, God—!

(PAULA *starts kissing* BEN. *Voices off. He disengages.*)

BEN: Careful! They're coming…

(*Enter* HAROLD , LORENZO , MARIA, MILLY, NICHOLAS, *and* PHILIP.)

LORENZO: Did you see *The Devil Wears Prada*? Why weren't you playing that role? Meryl Streep does everything. What is she doing now? Do you know?

MARIA: What? How should I know?! She's become a movie star. Though I hear she's going to do something or other on stage again—finally!—in the Park, or something. I don't really care. Is this going to start?

LORENZO: Same thing with Judi Dench…I mean what gives with—

MARIA: Where's Alex? Philip, sit with me.

MILLY: *(Lighting up and offering him one:)* Cigarette?

PHILIP: No, no it's such a disgusting habit! How can you smoke knowing what we know? It kills you. And second hand smoke is just as bad... *(He gets up.)*

MILLY: Not outside it isn't. It's fine.

(ALEX comes out from behind the stage.)

MARIA: Darling—?

ALEX: Everybody?! Sit anywhere! Just...anywhere!

MARIA: Darling, are you starting now?

ALEX: *(Tense)* In a minute, Mom. Just be patient! *GOD!!!* *(He goes back behind.)*

MARIA: My son, "I will sit like Patience on a monument, smiling at grief."

(LORENZO applauds. PHILIP sits next to her.)

MARIA: Darling...

(As people find their seats, ALEX returning:)

ALEX: May I have your attention, please?

MARIA: Yes! Yes! *(Applauding)* Attention! Attention must be paid!

ALEX: We're about to begin.

(More applause. He quiets them. A pause)

ALEX: Thanks... Okay. *(Long pause. He starts:)* ...Imagine, if you will, the earth...only decades from now— *(Pause)* ...Let the ocean's ghosts haunt you as you dream...

MARIA: Yes, let them haunt us!

ALEX: Mom! *(Pause)* ...Let sleep descend—

(Pause. Sound of waves, birds.)

(They all stare at the stage U S. No one is there.)

(Finally, NINA in white, climbs up the stairs D S from the ocean, dripping wet, speaking.)

(They all turn.)

NINA: Men, lions, eagles, bears; geese, antelope; tiny creatures invisible to man's eye—all forms of life—all life has ended…and become extinct. No living creature walks the earth. No gull cries on the shore of the sea, no owl hoots from its perch in the wood. The earth is silent… Cold… Empty… The oceans are dead. *(She walks towards the stage.)* The bodies of the living have turned to dust. That dust has turned to stone, to water, to clouds. *(She steps onto the stage, slowly turns.)* The souls of the living…have become one soul. …I am that soul. I am man. I am woman. I am beast. I remember all that was—glorious and venal—human and bestial—

MARIA: *(In a low voice)* Uh-oh. We're in for something naughty now…

ALEX: Mom!

NINA: I am alone. My voice echoes in the void, unheard… Man…has destroyed the earth…

(Pause—ALEX releases the stink bomb.)

NINA: Evil's stench pollutes the night air.

MARIA: What's that? Do you smell something? It smells like rotten eggs…or—or—

LORENZO: Is that sulfur?

MARIA: Something absolutely stinks! Is this in the script?

ALEX: Yes!

MARIA: Is it absolutely necessary?

ALEX: YES! IT'S NECESSARY!!!!

NINA: The cruel struggle// between man's greed and nature's—

(MARIA *coughs and chokes.*)

MARIA: Good God! (*Coughs and chokes*) It certainly is *effective*!

(*More coughing*)

NINA: The cruel struggle //

ALEX: Alright! That's it! (*Runs towards the stage*) The play's over! It's over!! ALL OVER! (*Gets* NINA *off-stage*) Well done, Mom. You totally fucked up my play. SATISFIED?

MARIA: What are you so angry about?

ALEX: How could I forget that YOU—only YOU and AND AND AND your stupid friends are good enough to write and act in fucking plays! You, you—GOD!! I—I just—HATE— (*He runs off.*)

MARIA: What's wrong with HIM? What did I say?

NICHOLAS: Maria, really. You can't embarrass a young man like that. He has his pride!

MARIA: What did I say?

NICHOLAS: Are you joking? You hurt his feelings! Deeply.

MARIA: But, really…I mean he told us earlier it wasn't supposed to be serious. I took it as a kind of joke.

NICHOLAS: Well, it wasn't.

MARIA: What then? It's supposed to be some kind of masterpiece, I suppose? A lesson, I'm sure, of some kind. God, how I hate self-important theater—self-righteous, preachy, pretentious nonsense that no one wants to hear. And these constant veiled or not so veiled critiques of me! He'd try the patience of a saint. He's a resentful, conceited little brat.

NICHOLAS: He only wanted to please you.

MARIA: Oh, really? Then why didn't he write a real play? With characters and scenes that were even vaguely entertaining?

PHILIP: We all write what we can and what we think we have to say.

MARIA: Well, what he has to say is that he is creating a whole new genre of theatre because everything I do is...crap. He's mean and...spiteful, and, and—

BEN: Your anger is like the wrath of Zeus! I feel we should all take cover! Where's the thunderbolt from Mount Olympus?

MARIA: *(Sulky)* I'm not a goddess. I'm a woman.

BEN: *(Drily)* You sure the hell are.

MARIA: And I'm not angry. I just get so upset with him! wasting his time like this... Oh, dammit! I didn't want to hurt my darling child's feelings. *(To* NICHOLAS*)* I was horrible, wasn't I?

NICHOLAS: Yes.

HAROLD: You know, people try to write about huge subjects like the end of the world and good and evil, and maybe Alex should just write about—well... ordinary people. I mean, even people like me can be interesting if you—

MARIA: Everybody just stop talking! It's so beautiful tonight. Listen! They're having a party down the beach. The music sounds glorious.

PAULA: Yes...

MARIA: *(To* PHILIP*:)* Darling, fifteen, twenty-five... who knows how many years ago?—before you were even born!—

(Laughter)

MARIA: There was singing and music and love-making every night all up and down the beach. Now the place is crawling with hedge fund operators, or whatever they're called, and producers and moguls—but in the old days, the houses were filled with talented people— artists and musicians and writers— There were house parties every weekend, sometimes for a month at a time in the summer—remember? —and guess who was the biggest Don Juan of them all, the man every woman longed for? He's still very charming of course, our darling friend Ben—but in the old days, he was *absolutely* irresistible! Am I right, everyone?

NICHOLAS: Oh, yes.

PAULA: *(Begins to sob)* Oh, God…

LORENZO: Sh—s-s-s-hh… Quiet.

PAULA: …I'm sorry. I just got sad, all of a sudden. It's amazing how fast it all goes—our lives….

MARIA: Yes…

(They all listen to the music down the beach. If possible, Imagine *by John Lennon)*

MARIA: John Lennon. *(Vaguely)* Huh… Oh, God, I feel so guilty about my darling boy. Why did I hurt him? I didn't mean to… I didn't! *(Calling)* Alex! Alex, darling!

MILLY: I'll go look for him if you want.

MARIA: Would you? You're a dear.

*(*MILLY, *exiting, calling:)*

MILLY: Alex! Alex!

*(*NINA *comes out from behind the stage, dry and dressed. Applause)*

NINA: I guess we're not going on?

NICHOLAS: Bravo! Bravo!

MARIA: Brava! Brava! Come here, dear, and sit by me. You were utterly spectacular. So … earnest… and you are so lovely—beautiful face, beautiful voice, beautiful figure. Enchanting. You're an angel. You must decide tonight to go on stage for the rest of your life and never look back.

NICHOLAS: Maria!

NINA: Really? Do you mean that? Oh, my God… Coming from you…

MARIA: Let me introduce you to the writer, Philip—

NINA: Oh, yes. I know. I've read everything you've ever written.

PHILIP: Really?

NINA: Yes, I think you're a genius. I—

MARIA: Don't say anything more. He's very shy, and he also might get a swelled head.

(Laughter)

NINA: (To PHILIP) It's kind of a…strange play, isn't it?

PHILIP: Yes, I didn't understand a word of it. But still, I liked watching it. You were very…sincere, and sweet and it looked beautiful—the moon and the ocean, and particularly you…

NINA: Thank you.

PHILIP: Still, there's nothing I like better than fishing. Sorry. I'd rather fish than go to the theatre or the opera or a museum or even read a good book. I'm a very simple man. I like simple things…

NINA: Really? But you must like creating your books– being swept away by your creations…

MARIA: Stop spouting clichés or he'll run away! Won't you, darling?

(Silence)

BEN: The angel of silence has descended.

NINA: I have to go.

MARIA: Where are you going? It's still early! I won't let you go.

NINA: My father will kill me if I come in late.

MARIA: Oh, what a bother. Well, it can't be helped, I suppose.

NINA: You have no idea how much I want to stay!

MARIA: Somebody should see you home.

NINA: *(Alarmed:)* Oh, no! That's fine.

NICHOLAS: Don't go!

NINA: I have to.

NICHOLAS: Not even one little hour?

(On the verge of tears:)

NINA: No, I can't!

NICHOLAS: Well… We will miss you terribly, dear. Come back soon.

NINA: *(Crying and waving)* Oh, thank you. I will. *(She exits quickly.)*

MARIA: That poor darling! …Do you know, I hear her mother left her father a fortune when she died, and he made a will leaving everything to his second wife?!— That poor child has nothing and her step-mother is an absolute harridan, a real horror—I've seen her—and I gather she despises Nina. How could anyone despise that little angel?

BEN: Well, let's be honest. Her father's a miserable shit.

NICHOLAS: Well, I better go, too. My legs are beginning to ache. This old age will be the death of me.

MARIA: You're too young for old age.

NICHOLAS: Dream on, my dear. It's just around the corner for you, too.

MARIA: *(Enormously put out:)* What are you *talking* about?! Philip?

(Dog barks madly. To LORENZO:*)*

NICHOLAS: Goddammit! Please unchain that dog! He keeps me up at night and—

LORENZO: I can't do that. Since you refuse to put in an alarm system or an electric gate, that dog's the only thing that keeps us from being robbed blind or murdered in our beds.

NICHOLAS: I'd rather be murdered in my bed! I'D GET A NIGHT'S SLEEP! It would be a blessing!!!

(As HAROLD, LORENZO, MARIA *and* NICHOLAS *go:)*

MARIA: We do not need to spend a fortune on alarms and gates. How many times do I need to tell you this? Just unchain the dog so my brother can sleep.

(Following off:)

LORENZO: I can't do it.

NICHOLAS: What was I thinking wanting to call this home? Can you tell me that?

HAROLD: Well, how much does an alarm system cost?

(They're gone. BEN *remains, listening to the party on the beach.)*

*(*ALEX *enters. Looks around)*

ALEX: Everyone's gone…

BEN: I'm here.

ALEX: Milly's been chasing me all over the beach. She's so—I don't know—bizarre…

BEN: Alex, I really liked your play.

ALEX: Really?!

BEN: Of course I didn't get to see or hear the whole thing, but it made a real impression on me. It affected me very deeply. In fact, I felt it just now when I was alone, looking out on the water…

(ALEX *hugs* BEN, *crying.*)

ALEX: Oh, thank you!

BEN: Well, it's true. You were going after something really important that needs to be said. Promise me you'll keep writing, Alex. I think you have an original talent.

ALEX: You do?!

BEN: Yes. Believe in yourself. And write what you want to write…

ALEX: Oh, God…

(BEN *sits.*)

BEN: You know, when I was your age, I wrote poetry—not plays—but I think now, if only—

ALEX: Where's Nina?

BEN: If only someone had encouraged me—

ALEX: Did she leave?

BEN: Yes, she's gone home.

ALEX: Oh, my God! Oh, my God! I have to go find her!

BEN: Calm down, Alex. She's probably home by now.

ALEX: No!!! No! I have to go after her!

(MILLY *enters.*)

MILLY: Alex, your mother wants to see you up at the house. She's very upset.

ALEX: Tell her I'm gone, forever! Jesus! All of you… Just leave me alone! (*To* MILLY:) And you! Stop following me! You make me crazy!

BEN: Calm down, Alex. It's alright.

ALEX: It's not alright! It will *never* be alright! Oh, my God! Ben! *(He hugs him impulsively, starts to cry)* I have to go. Oh, God…

(ALEX exits quickly.

(Pause)

BEN: Well, time for me to go up to the house, too, I suppose.

MILLY: Can I talk to you?

(BEN sighs.)

BEN: Why not? It seems to be the night for it.

MILLY: Well, I'm sorry to ask, but I just need some advice from someone who isn't completely crazy like everyone else around here. And—and I don't know why, but I've always felt close to you…

BEN: …Okay.

MILLY: And I'm afraid I'm going to do something so completely nuts and something that will so completely wreck my life, and I don't know if I can really stand it anymore…so…

BEN: Just tell me what's wrong, Milly.

MILLY: I'm… Nobody knows how much I'm dying inside, every day… *(Tears pouring)* I'm—I'm so in love with Alex.

BEN: Oh, dear God. I'm sorry, dear. I'm so sorry.

(Sobbing, MILLY runs into BEN's arms.)

MILLY: I know! What am I going to do? What am I—?

BEN: …There's nothing to do…

(MILLY sobs.)

BEN: Oh, my… All this love! All this painful love…

*(*BEN *holds* MILLY *as lights fade.)*

END OF ACT ONE

ACT TWO

(Mid-day. Hot. The beach. Umbrellas, beach chairs. The stage is still up.)

*(*BEN, MARIA, *and* MILLY, *reclining.* BEN *has been reading to them.)*

MARIA: *(To* MILLY:*)* Come on! Get up and stand next to me.

MILLY: What? Why?

MARIA: Just do it. Side by side.

*(*MILLY *groans and gets up.)*

MARIA: *(To* BEN:*)* Ben, which one of us looks younger?

BEN: *(Without looking up from the book:)* You do, of course.

MARIA: There! You see? He's absolutely right! You're twenty-two and I'm…almost twice your age, and I look younger than you. Now why is that?

*(*MILLY *looks at* MARIA *then shrugs.)*

MARIA: Because I'm active! —Because I'm passionately engaged with my life, and my work, and my art and I'm madly, blindly in love! That's what you need, Milly. To get passionately engaged in your own life. You just sit around all day in the same spot, doing nothing!

MILLY: I know, but…I'm so…tired… I feel like a dried-up old prune; I always have. Maybe I was born this way.

MARIA: Oh, nonsense! You would feel much better if you'd just put on some attractive clothes, washed and brushed your hair—or better yet, you know what you really need? A fabulous hair-cut—I'll take you to my stylist in the City. Ask your father to drive us in. I'll take you today.

MILLY: You will?!

MARIA: Absolutely. He goes on vacation tomorrow, so it has to be today. And then we'll go straight to my personal shopper at Saks and get you a new outfit. Maybe two! One for the party at the end of the month. God, I wish I'd had a daughter! I understand girls. I don't understand boys. I never did. Especially adolescent boys. I didn't understand them when I dated them, and I don't understand them now!

(BEN *laughs*.)

MARIA: (*Intimately to* MILLY:) You know, I'll share something with you, darling—woman to woman. Do you know I would never dream of leaving my bedroom—even to go downstairs to get my morning coffee—without first having showered, dressed, done my hair just so, and—most important, put on my make-up…*carefully*?

MILLY: Really?!

MARIA: *Yes.* All of us need a little help, dear, no matter how good-looking we are. You can't just roll out of bed and present yourself to the world unkempt and disheveled. When I was your age, I thought I could … but I was wrong.

(BEN *laughs*.)

MARIA: The sad truth is, dear, every woman needs a little make-up, no matter what her age. You must promise me you will *never* let yourself go like so many women do…I'll tell you another secret, dear. I still believe I can get any man I want—

(They giggle.)

MARIA: —truly! And believe me, that's half the battle. Oh. And yoga! I do it every morning. Look at me! *(She starts to skip down the beach, arms akimbo.)* I could still play Juliet!

BEN: *(Drily:)* Well, I'm going back to this book. We stopped at: "And yet they are very desirable…" I think I like what's coming.

(MARIA Snatches it away from BEN:)

MARIA: I'll read to us now! *(She sits back down.)* Ready? Where were we?

(MILLY lies back.)

MARIA: "And yet they are very desirable…" Oh, God, beach fiction…I can't believe we're actually reading this! At least it's French…We can pretend it's worthwhile… "And yet…" blah, blah, oh here. "When Anouk chose the man she wanted to possess, she showered him with compliments, coy looks, and *favors*…" Oh, please… How ridiculous. French women might think men don't see through that kind of behavior, but really!

BEN: What do you mean? It sounds okay to me.

MARIA: Ben! If an American woman gets her man it's usually because she's fallen madly in love with him. That's all. Look at me and Philip. I didn't shower him with compliments or "favors", or anything else!

BEN: Oh, no?

MARIA: No! I simply fell head over heels in love with him and he with me. In fact, sometimes I'd just look at him, and I'd start to cry—and I'd cry and cry and cry… just because I was near him—and he did the same.

BEN: Oh yeah. Right.

(Enter NICHOLAS *and* NINA *with* HAROLD.*)*

NICHOLAS: So are you having a good time finally? Are you happy that your father and stepmother have gone to the City? And you're free as a bird for three whole days?

*(*NINA *plops down next to* MARIA.*)*

NINA: Yes, yes, yes! I'm here where I belong!

MARIA: Yes! And nicely dressed, too—you see, Milly? A fabulous haircut and a perfect little dress and just a touch of…mascara? And do I detect a hint of blush?

NINA: Oh, I don't think so. I think that's all…just me…

MARIA: I see… Well, we mustn't praise you too much or you'll get hateful. Where's Philip?

NINA: He's down by the dock, fishing.

MARIA: Hmph. I'm surprised he isn't sick of it. *(Picking up the book:)* Now where was I?

NINA: What are you reading?

(Showing her the cover:)

MARIA: Some French romance.

HAROLD: Oh, right. I haven't read it. It's on the summer best-seller list, isn't it?

MARIA: Yes. It's trash.

BEN: Actually it would do you good to read it, Harold.

HAROLD: Really? Why?

BEN: It might get your blood pumping… What do you think, Milly?

HAROLD: Excuse me? I'm not sure what you're insinuating, but I am sure I don't—

MARIA: Stop it! Well, the rest looks boring and it's obviously wrong. (*She tosses the book*) …God, I'm so upset. What's the matter with my son? He's so depressed and I never see him any more.

MILLY: His heart's breaking. (*To* NINA:) Will you recite something from his play?

NINA: (*Shrugging:*) Why? It's so…weird.

MILLY: I don't think so. When Alex read it out loud, his eyes shone and the poetry just soared. It's magnificent. I think it's a brilliant play.

(NICHOLAS *snores. He's fallen asleep with his mouth open.*)

MARIA: Nicky!

(NICHOLAS *wakes up with a snort.*)

MARIA: Are you asleep?

NICHOLAS: Of course not.

MARIA: It's the middle of the day! You should see a doctor.

NICHOLAS: I don't get any sleep with that fu— infuriating dog! That's all.

BEN: I've told you, you need to get a check-up. I want you to get your blood results if nothing else. You shouldn't be so exhausted all the time.

MARIA: I have a great idea! Why don't we all go to a spa together? Wouldn't that be just too fun? We could all get massages, and eat healthy food, and get mud wraps, and salt rubs and we'd all sleep…like babies!…

BEN: Sure we could all do that. Better yet, why don't we just shoot ourselves?

MARIA: What is that supposed to mean?

BEN: Whatever you want it to mean.

HAROLD: Nicholas should just stop drinking so much. And smoking.

MARIA: *(Hurt)* Nobody listens to me.

BEN: Because you are an impossible woman! I want your brother to go to a doctor. This isn't about you!

(Hurt and injured:)

MARIA: I see.

NICHOLAS: None of you understands that all I want to do is live a little! You've all had wonderful lives and I haven't!

MARIA: Oh, stop it!

NICHOLAS: No, really! If I drink some good wine, or have a scotch before dinner or smoke a cigar after dinner, or even smoke a cigarette during the day, it isn't exactly drinking and smoking to excess!—and that's all the pleasure I have in my life, so LET ME HAVE IT!

MARIA: Okay!

BEN: To look back at your life at your age and piss and moan about what you missed is … well—

MILLY: Must be time for lunch!… *(She gets up and stumbles.)* Oops! My foot fell asleep.

(MILLY exits, weaving, towards the house. They watch her.)

BEN: She's going to knock off a couple more drinks before lunch, don't you think?

NICHOLAS: The poor thing. She's miserable! just like I was at her age, and chances are it's not going to get any better.

BEN: Oh, for Christ's sake, Nick!

(ALEX, *hoodie up, walks the beach in front of them.* MARIA *sees him.*)

MARIA: Alex, darling! Come here.

(ALEX *keeps walking, exits. Pause, then:*)

MARIA: God it's hot! And it's so quiet! I can't stand it! I'd so much rather be home in the City or in a hotel room anywhere in the world and be working, or preparing, or going over my lines before a performance, or anything but this! I HATE VACATIONS. I don't know how to take them and I hate them! I don't like to do nothing. I don't know HOW!

NINA: Yes, yes! Me, too! I'm just like you.

(MARIA *looks at* NINA.)

MARIA: Really…

NICHOLAS: We all know you're happier in the City, Maria, but this gives you time to be with your family. In the City you may have meetings, and theatre and rehearsals and WORK, but here you have the ocean, and the beach, and well, US! Don't you care about us, at all? Just for a few weeks a year, let it all go!

(LORENZO *enters with* PAULA *following, upset:*)

LORENZO: Who says they want me to drive them into the City today?

(*Waving her fingers:*)

MARIA: Me! I want to take your daughter in to have an appointment with my hairdresser immediately. (*Laughing*) Yesterday if possible. He'll see her today once I explain it's an emergency.

LORENZO: Well, it's impossible today, Maria.

MARIA: Pardon me?

LORENZO: I'm swamped with work! I can't possibly drive you in, wait for your beauty appointment and drive you back out at rush hour. The pool man is coming today—we are planting the front garden just as you requested—you have no idea how difficult it was to find the exact varieties and colors you asked for—the tent man is coming to inspect the grounds for the party, and—

MARIA: Well, have José…greet the tent-man and the gardeners, or whatever needs to be done with them.

LORENZO: José is doing work for me in the kitchen. We've just finished making lunch and we are starting the preparations for the evening.

MARIA: You are "starting the preparations for the evening"? I don't believe you! You're just making this up to—to drive me crazy! Don't you care about your daughter at all? This hair appointment could save her life!

LORENZO: *(A slow burn:)* …The best I can do to have you…chauffeured into New York is the beginning of next week. And since I, myself, am not a chauffeur I will have to arrange it so that José can be freed to drive you. But not today. Today is impossible, as I've explained. José is fully booked!

MARIA: I—I can't believe how I am being treated. Nothing I want seems to matter around here! Well… That's it! You have insulted me, just as you'd hoped. I'll go back to New York on the train, or I'll take the JITNEY! for God's sake! And I won't ever come back!!

LORENZO: Fine. In that case, I quit. Find someone else to abuse! *(He exits.)*

MARIA: Oh, God, oh, God, oh, God!!! I hate this!! It's the same thing every year. Why should I have to put up with this? I'm never stepping foot in this house again as long as he's here! *(She exits towards the boat house.)*

NICHOLAS: Oh… This is just outrageous. I am fed up with these people.

PAULA: I'm so sorry, Nicholas. I don't know what I can do. He's an impossible man. He always has been. Think of what I have to put up with every day!

NICHOLAS: He's leaving? Just leaving? *In high season*?! And before our party? He can't do this to us. I'll just march right up there and insist that he stay.

BEN: Oh, good going, Nick. Show some back-bone.

NICHOLAS: *(To* NINA:*)* Come on, let's go find Maria and beg her not to go.

*(*BEN *groans.)*

NINA: Oh, yes, let's! I just can't believe anyone would dare speak to…to Maria like that!

(As NICHOLAS *and* NINA *go:)*

NICHOLAS: Yes, isn't it awful, but he is not going to get away with it this time. I plan to give that man such a piece of my mind!

(They're gone.)

BEN: When did Nick turn into such a big baby?

PAULA: …Wasn't he always a big baby?…

*(*BEN *laughs.)*

BEN: …You're right. Nick should have fired your husband on the spot, but you know what's going to happen. Nick and Maria are going to end up crying and apologizing to HIM! and then they'll beg him or pay him tons more money to stay…

PAULA: God, I really can't stand any more. Can't you take me home with you? Let me leave him today and be with you. How many more years do we have to wait? What time is it, Ben?! We're getting old.

BEN: You're right. And now I'm too old to change.

PAULA: (*Stifling a sob:*) Wh—…I know you have other women. I understand that… It's alright! I'll put up with it as I always—

BEN: What?

PAULA: I'm sorry…I'm sorry I didn't realize…after all these years you're tired of me. Of course you are. I—

BEN: No, no…

PAULA: You were with Maria all morning, weren't you?

BEN: (*Irritated:*) Well, yes, I was with Maria all morning. So?

PAULA: I'm sorry, I'm so sorry. I just get so jealous. It's killing me.

BEN: I'm not tired of you, Paula.

PAULA: Really?

BEN: Really.

PAULA: (*Sobbing:*) Oh, thank God… (*Whispering, choked:*) If you have to be with other women, just don't let me see it, alright?

BEN: I'll do my best.

(NINA *appears with a bouquet of flowers.*)

BEN: How's it going up there?

NINA: Nicky is crying and Maria is having an asthma attack.

BEN: Oh…right… So…I'll go up and see what I can do.

(NINA *gives* BEN *the flowers.*)

NINA: These are for you.

BEN: Ah! *Muchas gracias, senorita!* *(He exits towards the house.)*

NINA: *(Giggling:)* De nada.

(PAULA follows.)

PAULA: What pretty flowers! Let me see them. *(Near the house in a low voice:)* Give me those flowers!

(PAULA tears them to pieces and dumps them as BEN and PAULA exit into the house.)

(ALEX enters with a dead seagull.)

ALEX: You're alone…

NINA: Yes.

(ALEX puts the dead bird at her feet.)

NINA: What's that supposed to mean?

ALEX: I was heartless enough to kill this bird…instead of myself. I lay it at your feet.

NINA: What's wrong with you?

ALEX: I'll kill myself like this, too. One day soon…

NINA: Where did you get a gun?

ALEX: Lorenzo keeps one in the kitchen. I took it.

NINA: I don't understand who you are anymore!

ALEX: I feel the same way about you. Who are you? You're cold, you hate being around me.

NINA: It's because you act so crazy. You talk in these… symbols. And this seagull! I mean, really. I'm sorry, but I just don't understand. I must be too stupid to understand you.

ALEX: It's not hard to understand, Nina. It all began the night my play…failed. Women don't forgive failure. Well…you'll be happy to know I tore it up, all of it. And then I deleted it. It no longer exists. Oh, Nina, you can't imagine how miserable I am! I'm so unhappy! I can't believe you stopped loving me! And I still adore you! My play was a disaster and now you despise me. You think I don't have any talent and I'm just pathetic and worthless... Oh, God, losing your love is so awful, it's so unbelievable, it's like I woke up one morning and the ocean had dried up or disappeared! Nina, Nina. I understand it all perfectly! Perfectly! and it's like a nail is being driven into my brain. The pain is unbearable! I adore you and you can't stand me...I'm dying.

(ALEX *sees* PHILIP *walking down the beach reading from a notebook as he walks.* NINA *sees him too and smiles.*)

ALEX: Oh, God, look who's here. He hasn't even seen you yet, and look at you! you're...melting. Oh...God... well, I won't get in your way. (*He exits quickly.*)

NINA: Good morning, Philip.

(*Looks up:*)

PHILIP: Oh, good morning. It seems we're leaving today—due to some "unforgivable behavior"...?

(PHILIP *makes a face.* NINA *laughs.*)

NINA: Yes. I was there.

PHILIP: Were you?

NINA: Yes. It was pretty...well, pretty awful...

PHILIP: (*Smiling:*) Was it?

NINA: Yes.

(*Long pause*)

PHILIP: You know, I don't often have the opportunity to meet young girls—interesting young women—and since I can't remember what it feels like to be eighteen or nineteen and since I never was a girl!

(NINA *giggles.*)

PHILIP: ...the young women in my stories always seem, well, unconvincing at best—sort of flat, and one-dimensional and...

NINA: No, they're not! That's not true at all.

PHILIP: Yes, my dear, I'm afraid it is true. What I wouldn't give to live in your shoes for just one hour and think what you think and feel, really feel, what you feel...

NINA: You have no idea what I'd give to be in your shoes, even for five minutes.

PHILIP: What? Really? Why?

NINA: Well, to feel what it's like to be a real writer? A famous writer...? Are you serious? How *does* it make you feel?

PHILIP: How does it make me *feel*? Well, it doesn't make me feel anything, to tell you the truth. I never think about it. Either you are exaggerating how famous I am or else being famous doesn't produce any particular feelings.

NINA: I don't believe you. Like how do you feel when you read about yourself in the newspaper?

PHILIP: When I get a good review, I'm relieved. When they say vicious and negative things about my work, I get depressed for a few days—and angry, I suppose, and then I get back to work. That's the only thing to do. Just do your work, regardless.

NINA: Oh, you are so great. You're so lucky to be so... happy, and noticed and smart!

PHILIP: God, you're young. So adorable, and so young.

NINA: Yes. Forgive me. I am young and curious and so...in awe of you. I can't believe I'm standing here talking to you, like I'm just talking to another person.

(PHILIP *laughs.*)

NINA: Do you ever think you're living some amazing dream?

PHILIP: Excuse me.

NINA: What?

PHILIP: *(Looking at his watch:)* I have work to do.

NINA: Did I say something wrong?

PHILIP: No. It's just…Well, you hit a nerve, I'm afraid, and I'm a bit irritated by how I'm feeling, that's all. And I need to get some work done.

NINA: Tell me why I've…irritated you.

PHILIP: Oh, I don't know…

NINA: Please?

PHILIP: Oh, alright. …You want to talk about what a "dream" my life is?

NINA: Yes!

(Pause)

PHILIP: Okay… Let's see… Do you have any idea what…obsession is, or compulsion?

(NINA nods.)

PHILIP: Alright. Well, the truth of the matter is, I'm not in control of my life. I'm obsessed by one thought: the same thought day and night – and that thought is: I should be writing. I should be writing. I should be writing. No matter what I'm doing, I should be writing. I could be having a glass of wine, or fishing, or making love or having dinner, alright? And my mind is telling me to stop doing what I'm doing because I SHOULD BE WRITING! What kind of dream life is that? It's more of a nightmare, don't you think? I can't enjoy my life because I don't allow myself to live it! In fact, I cannibalize it! I see a poor pathetic girl who is drinking herself and smoking herself to death, dressed

like a Goth and I don't comfort her or talk to her I take
NOTES! That's what I was just doing when I bumped
into you. Taking notes about Milly because I might
want to use the details of who she is in a short story or
a novel someday. I mean, come on! I'm not living. I'm
observing living. I am talking to you here and I look
up at the sky for a moment and notice the shape of that
cloud formation. Hmmm, I think. It's shaped like a
grand piano!

NINA: *(Laughing:)* Oh, totally…

PHILIP: I should make a note of that, or on the way here
I smelled honey-suckle. That would be a great way to
evoke a summer day—the too sweet smell of honey-
suckle. Oh, this just goes on forever and ever. It drives
me fucking crazy. It's like I'm devouring my own life.
And I have no real relationships, no real friends. Most
of the people I know, know me and hang out with me
because I'm famous, at least for the moment. I am sure
as soon as I'm out of favor with the critics, they'll drop
me and I won't be invited to any more dinner parties
or country houses until I'm in favor again—if that
happens in my life-time—and I'll be alone with my
goddamn compulsion to notate everything everyone
says, or looks like and I'll continue to write it all down
until the day I die, and then I'll wake up one day and
say, "oh, dear. I forgot to live". And it will be over.

NINA: *(Stunned:)* But don't you like to write at all?

PHILIP: Oh, sure. Sometimes. When it's flowing it feels
wonderful. It's almost as good as sex, actually. And
I like reading the galleys. But then it gets published
and my heart just sinks. Not because it's a failure, but
because it's so…puny. Why was I so obsessed? It's a
nice little story or a good little novel, but in the grand
scheme of things it absolutely *doesn't matter*. It adds
nothing to the canon. No one would have missed me

if I'd never lived or never written a thing. And that's very depressing, dear. I'm afraid when I die, I'll hardly merit an obit in *The New York Times*.

NINA: Oh, that's so not true! If you died, lots of people who never even knew you would be…in mourning!

(PHILIP *laughs*.)

PHILIP: You're so sweet. You almost make me happy.

NINA: You're just spoiled by all your success, that's all.

PHILIP: All my success??? What success? Haven't you been listening? I don't like myself. Nobody really cares about me. And my work isn't good enough. I feel I should be writing something serious, something of consequence about politics or our execrable foreign policy, or this insane war we're in, and I do speak out every once in awhile—in a feeble voice no one wants to hear—but the more I try to write a serious book, or a book of real consequence the more false and hollow it seems to be. I feel like I'm constantly falling behind my peers, like an old man running to catch a train, and I just see it vanish into the horizon without me. Don't you understand? I feel like a failure.

NINA: But that's impossible! You're probably just working too hard. You may not be happy with your books and stories, but most people think you're brilliant. Brilliant, and handsome, and you're adored by…anyone who knows how to read!

PHILIP: You're a darling child. You almost make me feel better.

NINA: If I could be an actress and achieve one tenth as much as you in my entire life-time—

MARIA: *(From the porch of the house:)* Philip!

PHILIP: …I'm being summoned…
I don't really want to go now.

NINA: Really? *(Long pause)* Do you see that house with the flag-pole and the garden in front— down the beach?

(PHILIP turns to look.)

PHILIP: Yes.

NINA: I grew up in that house. You've traveled all over the world, I know, but I've never really lived anywhere else. Maybe when I go to college next year—I'll go someplace far away…

PHILIP: …It's beautiful here. And peaceful. You're very lucky.

NINA: I am?

PHILIP: You have no idea… *(Spotting the dead bird:)* What's this?

NINA: Oh, Alex shot it. It's a seagull.

PHILIP: Huh.
Try to persuade Maria to stay. *(He starts to write something in his notebook.)*

NINA: What are you writing?

PHILIP: Just a note. You see? I can't stop myself.

NINA: Can you tell me what it is?

PHILIP: …It's an idea for a short story. A girl—like you—lives her whole life on the beach. She loves the ocean, like a seagull—she's happy and free—and then one day, a man comes along and for no particular reason—maybe just because he has nothing better to do—destroys her…like this seagull.

MARIA: Philip!! Where are you?!

(PHILIP starts up to the house.)

PHILIP: *(Calling:)* Coming! What is it?

MARIA: We're staying!

(PHILIP *turns around and looks at* NINA, *then continues up to the house.)*

NINA: *(To herself:)* Oh, my God. I can't believe this is happening to me.

END OF ACT TWO

ACT THREE

(Inside the house. The dining room. PHILIP *eating.* MILLY *sitting with him. Suitcases by the door. A week later.)*

MILLY: If he died, I wouldn't be talking to you. I'd be dead, too. I'm only telling you this because you're a writer and you could maybe…I don't know…use it. *(She pours a drink.)* I'm getting married, by the way.

PHILIP: Really?

MILLY: Yeah. To Harold. He's the best I can do.

PHILIP: You don't have to do that.

MILLY: Yes, I do. *(Drinks)* I've loved Alex for as long as I can remember and he hates me. I figure once I'm married, I can forget about love. I'll stop thinking about it. But, you know, it's still hard. It really, really…I don't know…I mean…hurts. *(She pours herself another drink.)*

PHILIP: Haven't you had enough?

MILLY: Nope. Don't look at me like that. *(She raises her glass.)* Sliante! I'm really bummed you're leaving.

PHILIP: Yes, well. I don't really want to go.

MILLY: Tell her you're staying.

PHILIP: No. We have to go. It's an impossible situation. First Alex tries to kill himself, then he tells Maria he's so mad he really wants to kill me, for some reason.

MILLY: Well, he's jealous. Duh... But that's none of my business.

(NINA *enters.*)

MILLY: You know, Harold isn't very bright, but he's a really good person and he adores me. And I feel sorry for him. Marrying him will make him really happy.

(LORENZO *comes in with more suitcases.* MILLY *gets up.*)

MILLY: Well, thanks for being my friend. When your new book comes out, will you send me a copy?

PHILIP: Sure.

MILLY: Inside write: "To my pal, Milly, who doesn't know what she's doing, or why she's here". Okay? See ya, Philip. (*She looks at* NINA *and exits.*)

(NINA *comes forward. Hands behind her back.*)

NINA: Shoot. Odd or even?

PHILIP: Odd.

(NINA *and* PHILIP *shoot.*)

NINA: Even. Too bad. I was trying to decide whether or not to become an actress. I wish someone would just tell me.

PHILIP: No one can tell you that. Just close your eyes and ask yourself: what do I want?

(NINA *gives* PHILIP *a little note.*)

NINA: I wrote you a note. At the end is a page number from your last book. Look at the last line on that page and think of me, okay?

PHILIP: You're very sweet.

NINA: Remember me?

PHILIP: I will. I'll picture you just like you were that day last week on the beach...when you were wearing a little white dress and there was a dead seagull on the beach…remember?

NINA: …Yes. I remember…

(Noises off)

NINA: …Look, try to see me alone for just two minutes before you go…

(NINA runs out. MARIA and NICHOLAS enter. LORENZO comes in to take the suitcases out to the car.)

MARIA: I'm telling you, Nicky. You should stay here. Someone should be here for Alex… *(To PHILIP:)* Who just ran out? Nina?

PHILIP: Yes.

MARIA: Well… Excuse me. I don't want to intrude.

PHILIP: *(Absently:)* No, no.

(MARIA sits.)

MARIA: I think I got everything packed, darling. I'm exhausted.

(PHILIP gets up.)

PHILIP: Is there a copy of *Nights And Days* anywhere?

MARIA: Look in Nicky's study, I put them all in the corner bookcase. He's read them all, haven't you, dear?

(NICHOLAS grunts. PHILIP exits.)

MARIA: Really, Nick. You really have to stay out here.

NICHOLAS: It'll be incredibly depressing once you're gone. What am I going to do with myself?

MARIA: Alex will be here and he needs you, darling. Someone has to take care of him now. We'll probably never know for sure why he tried to shoot himself, but I'm convinced the main reason is he's jealous of Philip and the sooner I get Philip away from here the better Alex will feel.

NICHOLAS: Maria, there are a lot of reasons why Alex is so unhappy. He is a smart and wonderful young man, but he's stuck out here with no money, no job and no future… He's ashamed of himself and he's so scared, Maria. I adore that boy and I think he cares about me, too, but I'm so worried about him and I don't know how I can help him. Really I don't.

MARIA: Yes, well, perhaps we can get him a job somewhere. Can't you get him like a—an internship or something in a local law office? Or, oh, I don't know…

NICHOLAS: The best thing you…or rather we…could do for him, I think, is to give him a little money so he can at least buy some decent clothes. If he could just put on a jacket and tie—he looks so shabby! and actually, I think he should travel—just get out of here—live a little—get his mind free of Nina and you and me and just find himself. Lots of young people do this and really, it just…saves a lot of them. I'm convinced of that.

MARIA: Oh, really! …Well, I mean, I can afford to give him money for some new clothes, of course, but *travel*? We have to stop spoiling him. He should get a job! Nicky, I'm not made of money! It's time Alex started to at least try to support himself. I mean, really. If he won't go to college, I think Alex should go into town after we leave and see if he can find a job, even at minimum wage.

NICHOLAS: No nephew of mine is going to be flipping burgers, Maria.

MARIA: Oh, please! It would do him good to work. Really work! (*She starts to cry.*) Nobody understands. I don't have a husband. I have no real security. Everything we have, I *earned*! And now everyone thinks I should just give it all away. While they just sit around!

NICHOLAS: I don't expect you to give it all away, darling. I know how hard you've worked, and saved, and how generous, really, really generous you are to all of us. I'm just worried about your son, that's all. This is a very tricky moment, Maria. Perhaps he should…see someone. I mean really see someone—a good therapist, two or three times a week, or…

MARIA: Well, yes. And I can pay for that, Nicky. Really. I will. But it's a miracle I've made as much money as I have! I'm an actress!

NICHOLAS: You're a darling, is what you are, and I'm sorry I'm such a burden, dear. I never could save anything. I've put everything into this stupid house. If I'd invested prudently instead of throwing it all away we'd have millions, and instead I tried to time the market and invested in plays that never went anywhere…

MARIA: I know.

NICHOLAS: And…oh, God, I'm sorry. I'm a fool and I apologize for it, but, oh, Jesus! I feel odd. Oh, God, my head is spinning and… (*Holding onto the table:*) Maria, I feel faint.

MARIA: (*Trying to support him*) Help! Help! Alex! Uncle Nicky's fainting!

(ALEX *enters, bandage on his head, with* HAROLD.)

MARIA: He's fainting.

(NICHOLAS *stumbles to a chair and sits.*)

NICHOLAS: It's okay, it's okay. I'm alright. I just got a little dizzy, that's all.

ALEX: Don't get crazy, Mom. He gets dizzy a lot. It'll pass. Uncle Nick! Why don't you lie down?

(*Long pause*)

NICHOLAS: Yes, yes. I will. I'll go lie down for a minute, but get me up before you go, Maria. Remember I'm coming with you.

(MARIA *sighs. Sits*)

HAROLD: I'll take you to your room, Nick.

NICHOLAS: I can get to my room by myself, thank you.

HAROLD: Okay. Then I'll just follow you.

NICHOLAS: Why??

HAROLD: Because I'll feel better knowing you're okay.

NICHOLAS: Oh, God…

(HAROLD *and* NICHOLAS *exit.*)

MARIA: He really scared me…

ALEX: It's not good for him to live out here, Mom. He's really depressed. If you could survive lending him even a little money, he could live in the city for awhile, and—

MARIA: I don't have that kind of money, Alex. What do you want me to do, sell the house? It's you and your uncle who want to live out here. I'm an actress. Not a banker. (*A pause*) And it isn't everyone's God-given right to… retire! Why do most men think it is?!

(*Pause*)

ALEX: Mom, will you change my bandage?

MARIA: Oh…alright… (*She goes to the sideboard and gets the gauze and necessary medical supplies.*) Sit down. (*She starts to unwind the bandage and starts to laugh.*) You look like you're wearing a turban! Yesterday a man in town asked me what your 'nationality' was. I told him you're a Sikh. I think he thought you were a terrorist!

(ALEX *and* MARIA *laugh.*)

MARIA: Alex, when I'm gone you promise me you won't…play with any…guns…

ALEX: I promise. Oh, God, Mom…I was just completely out of my mind…I was just so crazed and unhappy and for that one moment I just couldn't control myself. It won't happen again. Don't worry. I'm… Oh… Your hands feels so good and gentle, and— *(Pause)* Mom, do you remember when I was a little kid and you were in some play on Broadway, and we were staying in an apartment on the Upper West Side, and it had a courtyard and there was a fight in the courtyard one night, and the cleaning lady who cleaned for us got beat up and you—remember you took her in with her three kids and you plunked all the kids into our bath tub and cleaned them up and told them all stories?

MARIA: I did?

ALEX: Yeah. They loved it. Don't you remember?

MARIA: No. *(Putting on a new bandage)* I don't…

ALEX: And two ballet dancers lived next door. They used to come over for coffee a lot…

MARIA: Yes, I remember them!

ALEX: They were really skinny and they smoked all the time.

(Shaking her head:)

MARIA: …Dancers…

(A pause)

ALEX: Mom…these last few days when you've been taking care of me, I've loved you so much, just like when I was a little kid. So completely. I used to worship you, you know, and you adored me, and petted me, and spent time with me… We used to laugh and talk for hours… *(He starts to sob.)* Mom, I don't have anyone but you now. Why do you let that complete ass-hole get between us?

MARIA: Alex, you just don't understand him. He's a really good person.

ALEX: Oh, right! When somebody told him I was so mad I wanted to kill him, all he could think of was getting out of here as fast as he could. He wouldn't even talk to me.

MARIA: That's not true. I asked him to leave. You may not like our relationship, but Alex, please respect my right to…love him.

ALEX: I respect your right to love whoever you want, but you have to respect my right to say what I think of the guy. Philip's a real jerk, Mom. As far as I can tell, he knows how to do two things well—drink and fuck around with other women. He's not a nice man, Mom; you deserve better. Just open your eyes! The two of us are in here having a fight over him while he's in the other room probably hitting on Nina—trying to impress her with what a genius he is and—

MARIA: Do you enjoy hurting me? Do you? I respect Philip and I have to insist that you not say hideous things about him to my face.

ALEX: Well, I wish he respected *you*, and I'm sorry, Mom. I wish for your sake I could respect him, but I'm afraid I *can't*. I know you want me to think he's a genius like you do, but I think his writing is at best insignificant and at its worst, it quite frankly sucks.

MARIA: That's just envy, Alex. I'm sorry. People with no talent always try to put down successful people. I thought better of you than this.

ALEX: No talent? No talent? Is that what you think of me? I—I—I have more talent than the two of you put together! I have more talent in my little finger

than—than— *(He rips off the bandage.)* You two write
and act to please boring, middle-class narrow-minded
ass-holes and you suck up to critics so those talentless
mediocrities will write nice things about you and
you can make money and get famous for the—the—
garbage you two create. You even believe your
own pathetic good press when what you do has no
substance, no merit, and doesn't matter one tiny little
bit to the rest of humanity! I don't believe in you and I
don't believe in him!

MARIA: You little...bastard!

ALEX: Oh, go back to your stupid boyfriend and your
stupid, mindless, boring plays.

MARIA: I do not act in stupid, mindless b-boring plays!
Stop this! What do you think you're doing? Who do
you think you're talking to? You can't even write a
little one-act!

ALEX: You fucking miser!

MARIA: You little ingrate! You're a moocher, a sponger.

(ALEX starts to cry.)

MARIA: You pretentious, untalented little... critic! Oh,
Alex! Don't cry, oh, please don't cry! *(Starts kissing
him)* I didn't mean it. Oh, God, forgive me. I love
you, darling. I'm so sorry. I'm just so unhappy. Oh,
Alex, I know he's a bad boyfriend...but he's the only
boyfriend I've got... Please, try to understand. I love
you so much, darling.

(ALEX hugs MARIA.)

ALEX: Oh, Mom, I've lost everything. She doesn't love
me anymore! And, and I can't write...I know I can't!
And everything I hoped I'd be and everything I hoped
I had is just...gone! I'm dying...!

MARIA: It's going to be alright, sweetheart. You'll see. I'll get him out of here and she'll love you again and… stop crying…everything will be okay. Right? Right? Have we made up? Do you know how much I love you?

ALEX: Yes…

MARIA: We love each other again. Right? Right?

(ALEX *nods. Pause)*

MARIA: Make up with him, too, okay?

ALEX: No! I can't even look at him. Don't make me go near him. It's too…

(*Enter* PHILIP, *flipping through his book.)*

ALEX: I'm going. (*Exits quickly)*

PHILIP: "If you ever need my life, come and take it."

MARIA: What?

PHILIP: Oh, nothing. Just a line of mine I was looking for.

MARIA: You're all packed, I hope…

PHILIP: Huh… It's a nice line "If you ever need my life…" Hmph.

MARIA: The car should be here soon. I ordered a town car. It's so much easier than— (*She looks at him.)*

PHILIP: Let's stay one more day, darling.

(*Agitated:)*

MARIA: Sweetheart…I know why you want to stay. Please just try to have a little…self-control.

PHILIP: No, no, please. It isn't what it looks like… Just… Well, be a real friend. Let me just do this. I'll— I'll be back!

MARIA: Are you so…infatuated with her?

PHILIP: I guess I am. Darling, try to understand. This may be just what I need right now.

MARIA: Philip! She's an eighteen year old small-town girl! She's a child! What are you thinking?

PHILIP: Just trust me on this, Maria. I need her. I feel… I don't know…just something I've never felt before. I have to find out what it is. I don't want to die not knowing what this feels like. It's better for us, too, dear. I'd resent you forever if you denied me this.

MARIA: Oh, Philip, don't do this to me. I'm an ordinary woman. Don't talk to me like this.

PHILIP: You aren't an ordinary woman, darling. You are an extraordinary woman and a great artist and you know a love that's so sweet and so young and so innocent—it just takes my breath away. Nothing on earth could be so divine, so beautiful as this young, young love and I need to know what it is. I never had it when I was young. Let me have it now, darling, please. It's my last chance. Let me have it and then I'll come home to you, I promise.

MARIA: Have you completely lost your mind?!

PHILIP: Maybe. I don't really care.

MARIA: Everyone is conspiring to torture me today. *(She starts crying.)*

PHILIP: You just don't want to understand.

MARIA: Am I so old and hideous that you can talk about being madly in love with another woman right to my face? What do you think I'm made of? Philip, I adore you. You are my insane, handsome, brilliant glorious lover. My joy, my love…the last chapter of my life! *(Kissing him)* Don't desert me, darling, tell me you won't leave me. I can't live without you, darling, you know the passion of a real woman's love, you can't trade that for a child's…

PHILIP: Someone might come in...Maria...

MARIA: I don't care. Let them see how much I adore you, how much you love me...how we can't control how much we want one another. I'm not ashamed. Oh, my darling you want to do something crazy but I won't let you. I won't...let you... *(Laughing and kissing)* You're mine. You always will be. You are my glorious, talented lover, the most brilliant writer in the country, and you're *mine*—your eyes, your mouth, your hands are *mine*. Nobody understands or appreciates you the way I do, nobody. I am the only one who tells you the truth about yourself and understands your genius.

(PHILIP responds, kissing MARIA, brings her passionately to the ground, then stops)

PHILIP: You rob me of any will I thought I ever had... Alright...take me away, dear, but don't let me— don't ever let me out of your sight...do you promise?

MARIA: Whatever you say, darling... You know, if you want to stay, stay, darling. Whatever you want.

PHILIP: No, no. No... We'll just—we'll go together.

(As MARIA and PHILIP straighten themselves up, she calls in the next room.)

MARIA: We're ready! Is the car packed?

LORENZO: *(Off)* It just arrived. We're packing the big bags.

MARIA: Come in! Come in! The rest of the bags are in here!

(PHILIP is writing in his notebook.)

MARIA: What are you writing?

PHILIP: Oh, nothing. Just something I heard this morning that might come in handy, that's all.

(LORENZO enters and picks up two of the bags.)

LORENZO: Well…the hour has come, sadly, when you must leave us. I can hardly bear the thought of your departure, but there it is…Paula and I will be sure to contact all the people you were inviting to your party next week. I'll let them know…something came up…

MARIA: Something urgent, unavoidable…

LORENZO: Yes, something urgent and unavoidable has made you have to return to the City, and I will send each of them your very best wishes.

MARIA: No, no, send each of them all my *love*…

LORENZO: Of course…

(PAULA *enters behind him with a basket.*)

MARIA: I got you some plums from the market this morning to bring with you in the car. They're so sweet this year.

MARIA: Thank you, dear. How thoughtful…

PAULA: Forgive me if things weren't quite the way you wanted them…I—I—try so hard… (*She starts to cry.*)

MARIA: Oh, nonsense! It was perfect! Everything was just perfect, dear. As always.

PAULA: Where does the time go, Maria? It's all gone by so fast. It seems only yesterday when you first came out here with Alex. He was just a little boy! …Where have our lives gone?

MARIA: Yes, well… We're off! Good-bye, dear! Stay well! Where's Alex? I want to say good-bye. Tell him I'm leaving.

PAULA: Of course, I'll try to find him.

LORENZO: Don't forget to call.

MARIA: How can I forget to call?

(LORENZO, MARIA, PAULA *and* PHILIP *exit. Noises off. All follow.*)

(Stage empty. PHILIP *comes back, calling off:)*

PHILIP: I forgot my notebook. I think I left it on the table!

*(*NINA *enters.)*

NINA: I knew I'd see you again.

PHILIP: Oh. It's you. We're just going.

NINA: I've made a decision. I am going to be an actress. I'm moving to New York…I'll be where you are tomorrow.

PHILIP: *(Looking around, scribbling on his pad:)* Stay at this hotel. I'll pay. Call me the minute you arrive. This is my number. I have to go.

(Pause)

NINA: Just one more minute…Philip—

PHILIP: Dear God, you're beautiful. I can hardly believe I'll see you so soon! Your beautiful eyes, your mouth, your beautiful, beautiful angelic face…oh, my God.

(A long kiss.)

END OF ACT THREE

ACT FOUR

(Two years later. The dining room. ALEX*'s writing—his computer, printer, books and manuscripts—are on the dining room table. The couch is now a sleeping couch with bedding. Evening. Cold. Raining. The surf is roaring.* ALEX*'s stage can be seen out the window. What remains of the white curtain flaps in the wind.)*

(Enter MILLY *and* HAROLD.*)*

MILLY: *(Looking around:)* Nobody's here. That's odd. I wonder where Alex went? Maybe he went to find Nick.

*(*HAROLD *takes off his wet things.)*

MILLY: You know, they're inseparable now. Nick even wants to sleep in here while Alex is writing! He can't seem to live without him.

HAROLD: He doesn't want to feel alone. I understand that. *(He goes to the window, looks out.)* What horrible weather. Two full days of rain.

MILLY: The surf's roaring.

HAROLD: Yeah... Why didn't they pull that stage down? It looks so weird out there, like a skeleton— *(He laughs.)* Last night when I was walking over, I thought I heard somebody crying.

MILLY: Did you see who it was?

HAROLD: No...I don't think anyone was really there. I think...oh, never mind. *(A pause)* Let's go home.

MILLY: I'm going to stay over here again tonight. I told you that. I don't know why you bothered to walk over—especially in this weather! Why didn't you phone?

HAROLD: Don't you want to see the baby? It's been two days.

MILLY: Your sister told me she'd feed him.

HAROLD: The baby needs his mother, Milly.

MILLY: Stop it! Can't we even have a regular conversation anymore without you nagging me? All you can say is baby/home, baby/home, baby/home! You're making me crazy!

HAROLD: Let's go, Milly. Now. I mean it.

MILLY: You go. *(She gets up and gets a drink.)*

HAROLD: Your father won't drive me, and I didn't walk all the way over here to walk all the way back alone.

MILLY: I'll ask him. I'm sure he'll drive you.

(Long pause)

HAROLD: Are you coming home tomorrow?

MILLY: Maybe. *(Looks at him)* Okay! I don't know! Yes! Alright! Tomorrow.

(MILLY drinks. PAULA and ALEX enter with bedding.)

MILLY: What's all this?

PAULA: Fresh linens for Nicholas… He wants to sleep in here again tonight.

(ALEX helps PAULA with the bed.)

MILLY: I'll help you.

(PAULA leaves ALEX and MILLY to do it.)

PAULA: Old people are just like little children. Now I think he's afraid of the dark!

HAROLD: Well…I'm going.

(MILLY *doesn't look up.*)

HAROLD: 'Bye, Milly. 'Bye, Mother.

PAULA: Oh, just go already!

HAROLD: 'Bye, Alex. (*He exits.*)

PAULA: (*Looking at the manuscripts:*) Alex, nobody ever thought you'd become a real writer. But look at you! …Magazines are paying money for your short stories and you have an advance for writing a book…I'm so proud of you, dear… And you've gotten so handsome… (*Quietly:*) Alex…try to be kind to Milly.

MILLY: Mother! Stop!

PAULA: All a woman wants is a little kindness.

(ALEX *exits.*)

MILLY: Oh, God! Look what you've done! Just stay out of this, will you?

PAULA: I feel so bad for you, Milly. It's just…I know what you're going through…I—

MILLY: Well, I don't want to hear about it okay? (*She sits and starts to cry.*) It's just so stupid! This isn't supposed to happen in real life. This is what you read about in books! —It's sickening. Pathetic. I can't believe I've let this…obsession…ruin my life.

PAULA: I know, dear.

MILLY: Well, Harold got a job closer to the City. We're moving. We're finally going to leave his horrible family and get our own little house. He's going to be teaching seventh grade science in Woodmere. It's great. It's far away. He got great benefits, and maybe if I don't see Alex, I'll forget about him…

(*Music playing off:*)

PAULA: That's Alex playing his mother's old records. He's so depressed, too.

MILLY: If I can't see him, I know I'll be able to get over him. I'm sure. It's like quitting smoking. I'm going to do that, too. Cold turkey. Just STOP.

(Enter HAROLD *and* BEN *holding* NICHOLAS*'s arms on either side.)*

HAROLD: That's easy for you to say—you're loaded!

BEN: Loaded?! After thirty years practicing medicine— do you know how much money I have? I'm a small town doctor with a rich clientele only two months out of a year, and the H M Os are killing me! I've been able to save maybe a hundred thousand dollars all in. Seriously. So I took myself to Europe last year, and I spent a lot of money, and I'll go somewhere else again this year. And that's how it will be. I'll never be able to retire.

MILLY: *(To* HAROLD*:)* Harold, are you still here?!

HAROLD: Your father won't drive me. Nobody will drive me.

MILLY: Oh, for Christ's sake.

BEN: So…you've made a lot of changes since I've been here I see.

*(*PAULA *turns away.)*

BEN: You've turned the dining room into a what? study *cum* bedroom…?

MILLY: Alex likes to write in here and Nicholas wants to sleep near him, so…yeah. I guess…

NICHOLAS: Where's my sister?

BEN: She went to the station to meet Philip. He took a late train.

NICHOLAS: Huh. Well, you sent for my sister; I'm sicker than I thought. That's peculiar. I'm very ill; no one's given me any new medication, and I haven't heard of any plans to take me to the hospital. So…does that mean you're letting me die at home?

BEN: Nobody's dying! Least of all you. You'll outlive us all.

NICHOLAS: Crap. (Looking at the made-up couch) Is this for me?

PAULA: Of course it's for you.

NICHOLAS: Thank you very much. Where's Alex? I have another idea for him, for a short story—The title is: "The Man Who Wanted to Be Dot Dot Dot" …What do you think? When the man was young, he wanted to be a writer, but he couldn't write. When he was a lawyer, he wanted to be a brilliant litigator, to light up the courtroom with his eloquence and style, but he was terrified of going to trial, terrified of public speaking. Flop sweat, choking, the whole bit. He wanted to get married, but he never did… He wanted to live in the City, and he ends up dying in the country, and so on…

BEN: You wanted to be State's Attorney and you were.

NICHOLAS: No, no. That *happened* to me.

BEN: *Life* happens. It's really a drag to hear you complain about the unlived life, Nicky, and you've done it ever since I've known you!

NICHOLAS: Don't you understand? I want to live. I always wanted to experience—really *experience*—life. Why do you refuse to understand that?

BEN: Well, I DO understand, but we all have to die. Sometime.

NICHOLAS: Just wait. When it's your turn, you'll be afraid to die, too.

BEN: You know, I've watched a lot of people die in my life, but when the time really comes, the only ones I knew who were really scared of dying believed in heaven and hell. They were scared of meeting their Maker because they had lived incredibly sinful lives! But you—Nicky—I'm sorry. In the first place, you don't believe in God. And in the second place, what sins did you ever commit?! You spent thirty-five years in court… and unfortunately, that's about it…

NICHOLAS: I know…thrity-*eight*, but who's counting.

(BEN *and* NICHOLAS *both laugh. Enter* ALEX. *He sits near* NICHOLAS. MILLY *cannot keep her eyes off him.*)

BEN: We're keeping Alex from his work.

ALEX: It's okay.

(Long pause)

HAROLD: Doctor, what was your favorite city in Europe?

BEN: Rome.

ALEX: Rome. Really? Why?

BEN: It's so full of life! When you leave your hotel at night…you step outside and the streets are just full of people—walking, taking an evening stroll… Some are hand in hand or arm in arm, talking and laughing… they pass by beautiful new shops, gorgeous old plazas and fountains…ancient ruins, just as their ancestors did. It's a city with a soul—a universal soul…like in Alex's play… *(Long pause)* How is… Nina these days, Alex? Do you know?

ALEX: Fine I guess.

BEN: I've heard she's had… a hard time. Is that true?

ALEX: It's a long story.

BEN: Well, give me the short version.

(Pause. It's hard for him to talk about. After a sigh:)

ALEX: …She ran away from home and…lived with Philip. You probably know that.

BEN: Yes.

ALEX: Then, uh…I hear she got pregnant and lost the baby and he…lost interest in her, I guess, and left her and went back to his…old…relationship… Actually, he'd never really given up his old relationship. …He was seeing both women at the same time. The entire time… He—he… *(He won't say what he thinks of him.)* From what I hear, Nina's life is pretty much…a total disaster…

BEN: …Is she acting?

ALEX: Yes. Not in very good parts. Not in very good theaters either. I used to go see everything she did. I'd wait for her after the show at the stage door, but she'd never see me and I suppose I understand why, but after awhile, I just…had to…stop.

BEN: Is she good? She showed such promise.

ALEX: Is she good? I don't know. Not really. I mean, she never got any training. She's still beautiful and she's very sincere, and she always has great moments, but it comes out all awkward and her voice is bad and…don't ask me. She used to send me these friendly little e-mails, but she stopped doing even that after awhile, and I have no idea how she's doing. Her parents have basically disowned her. She isn't allowed at the house even. *(A beat)* She's here now, you know.

BEN: What? You mean she's—

ALEX: Yes, she's staying in town, down at the inn. She's been here a few days. I've gone down there to try to see her, but she won't see me. At the desk they say she won't see anyone…

HAROLD: I saw her walking on the beach road day before yesterday, I think, going towards town. I stopped her and asked her how she was and to come see us, and she said she would.

ALEX: Well, she won't.

(Pause)

NICHOLAS: She was such a beautiful girl. Angelic. I think I was a little in love with her.

BEN: You dirty old man…!

(NICK laughs. Noises off)

PAULA: It sounds like they're back from the station.

ALEX: Yes, I hear Mom.

(First from off then enter MARIA and PHILIP, followed by LORENZO.)

LORENZO: What is it with you, Maria? You never age!

MARIA: Stop it! You're a liar! And a terrible man!

(They laugh. She enters and kisses NICHOLAS.)

PHILIP: What are you doing still in bed, Nicholas? That's very naughty of you. *(Seeing MILLY:)* Milly! How are you?

MILLY: You remember me?

PHILIP: Of course I remember you. Did you get married?

MILLY: Yes.

PHILIP: Are you happy?

(MILLY gives PHILIP a look. He goes tentatively to ALEX.)

PHILIP: Your mother tells me you've forgiven me, Alex, and you're not angry any more. I hope that's true.

(No answer)

MARIA: Philip brought you your story in the *Ontario Review*, Alex!

(MARIA *hands it to* ALEX.)

ALEX: *(To* PHILIP:*)* Oh, thank you. That's very thoughtful of you.

(*He takes it from his mother.*)

ALEX: Did you like it?

PHILIP: Your admirers—and there are many, send their regards. People in New York are very interested in your work. They always ask me about you—what you look like, how old you are… For some reason, they think you're…old! or older than you are, and of course since nobody knows your real name, you're very mysterious. Smart move, my friend. Your… pseudonym is on everybody's lips!…

(*Laughter.*)

ALEX: Will you be here long?

PHILIP: Oh, no. I have to go back to New York tomorrow. I have a dead-line to meet on my new novel and an anthology to deliver. You know, same old story… *(He sits, shivers.)* God! The weather is awful. I'd hoped to do some fishing. Maybe if the wind dies down…? *(To* ALEX:*)* And I wanted to look around the beach where your play was done. I want to look at the location again, just to refresh my memory…

BEN: The stage is still up, Philip. *(He gestures to the window.)*

PHILIP: Oh, yes…I see. *(He goes to the window, looks out.)*

MILLY: *(To* LORENZO:*)* Dad, can you please drive Harold home? It's pouring.

LORENZO: I'm not going out again.

MILLY: Then can I drive him?

LORENZO: I need the car here, just in case…

MILLY: In case of what?…

LORENZO: He can walk.

HAROLD: Right. I can walk. Milly, just leave it. I'll walk.

PAULA: Walk…? In this weather? *(She shoots her husband a look.)*

HAROLD: Well… 'Bye, everyone. Sorry to be a bother, it's just the baby, and… Well, 'bye. *(He exits.)*

LORENZO: He'll be fine.

(MARIA spying the game on the sideboard)

MARIA: Look! The old Scrabble game we used to have when we were kids. Nicky, remember? Alex! Let's play a game before supper. *(To PHILIP:)* Philip darling, do you know how to play? *(She sits at the table and starts setting it up.)*

PHILIP: No, but it's a word game, isn't it?

MARIA: Alex used to be the best one in the family! He beat us all, from the time he was nine years old!

(ALEX kisses his mother on the top of her head as he exits with the magazine.)

MARIA: Alex, darling, aren't you going to play with us?

ALEX: No, thanks. I don't feel like it. I think I'll take a walk or something.

MARIA: But it's raining!

(ALEX is gone.)

MARIA: Alright. Everyone pick your partner. Ben, team up with Paula.

(All find a seat around the table, shoving ALEX's papers to the side as they do.)

MARIA: Philip, do you want to be my partner?

PHILIP: I'll try it on my own, thanks.

MARIA: Okay…Nicky darling, I'll be your partner.

NICHOLAS: I don't want to play.

MARIA: I want you to play.

(NICHOLAS *grunts.*)

MARIA: Come on, darling. Has everybody picked their tiles?

(*They do.*)

MARIA: I guess Milly goes first… She got an A!

(*They all look at everyone's letters, seeing the order, then pick their own and concentrate on their letters.*)

MARIA: I must tell you about the reception I got on the new play in Chicago. It's written by a young woman… very talented, I think, and directed by a young woman as well. You know, I haven't worked with many women directors before, but she's very bright and very…committed and I got a standing ovation on my individual bow, opening night. They made me take three calls! I was so moved, I just…well…I cried like a baby…

(*Pause*)

MILLY: There, 34 with the double word score…

MARIA: 34!? That's impossible! How did you do that?! And so fast?

PHILIP: Genius.

(*Laughter. All concentrate again.*)

MARIA: They have such good designers in these resident theatres, you know. The costume designer for my show won a Tony award last year, and you should have seen the fabrics he used on my second act dress. He actually had the silk imported from Paris, and I must say the dress was absolutely divine.

BEN: We can only get twelve.

PAULA: *(Giggling:)* That's so pathetic, Ben…

BEN: We have terrible letters! It's the best we can do. Alright, you try. Go ahead.

(Music off [Bach unaccompanied cello])

PAULA: That's Alex…playing your old records again, Maria. He's terribly depressed these days.

LORENZO: Well, he got a terrible mention in the *Atlantic*. What do you expect?

MARIA: Who cares about critics? It's the audiences that matter.

PHILIP: He hasn't found his voice yet, that's all. His stories are strangely intellectual. His characters don't *live*.

PAULA: I can only get a six. …

BEN: Right. So.. just go with the twelve like I said.

(She laughs sheepishly.)

PAULA: Of course, you're right.

MARIA: Nicky, that's a twelve. *(Looking at him)* Are you bored already? *(A pause)* He's asleep!

(Laughter)

PHILIP: You know…if I lived like this in a house on the beach, I would never write another word. I'd do two things—fish and play games. It is absolute bliss here.

BEN: Well, I believe in Alex. I think he's got a very special talent. He thinks in images—passionate, deeply felt images. He still needs to go beyond those images, maybe, but I think he is really, really exceptional. And he's young. I hope you're proud of your son, Maria. He's a real writer.

MARIA: What? *(Guiltily:)* You know, it's terrible, but I've never actually read a thing he's written. I just haven't had the time... *(Putting down a word)* Twenty-six!

(ALEX enters.)

MARIA: Oh Alex, come here and help me and Uncle Nick. We're losing.

(ALEX sits near his mother at the table.)

LORENZO: Philip! I've still got something of yours that you left here.

PHILIP: Oh, really? What?

LORENZO: You asked me to stuff a seagull Alex shot on the beach a couple of years ago.

PHILIP: Did I? I don't remember that.

(ALEX gets up. Goes to the French door, opens it, looks out)

ALEX: It's so dark out there!

MARIA: Will you shut the door, darling? I'm cold.

PHILIP: Oh, my God! Look! Triple word score, and I've used all my letters. Did I win?

MARIA: Oh, my God! You...21, 33, 36...108...plus 50. *(She kisses him.)* You are amazing...

LORENZO: Bravo. Supper's ready, if you'd like it now.

MARIA: Yes, let's eat. We can finish the game after dinner. Nicky darling, supper. We'll finish the game after supper. We mustn't let Philip go to bed with a swelled head...so to speak... We mustn't let him win! Alex, darling! Are you coming?

ALEX: No, thanks. I don't want anything. I'm not hungry.

(They all go in. noises off.)

(ALEX *alone. He picks up a hard copy of his manuscript.
Preparing to write, he reads through what he has already
written. He puts down one page with an impatient slam and
looks a few pages further in. He puts it down, despondent.
He clearly hates what he's written. He goes over to the
side board, and picks up a book from a huge stack and goes
back to his writing table, sits, looking for a passage in the
book. There is a tap on the window. He gets up, goes to the
window. No one. He opens the door leading to the beach.*)

ALEX: *(Calling:)* Who's there? *(He walks out further
towards the beach and the stage.)* Nina! Nina, is that you?

NINA: *(In a whisper:)* Yes.

(ALEX turns, sees NINA and grabs her.)

ALEX: Oh, my God…Nina, Nina, oh, my God, it *is* you.
I knew it would be…I could feel you out here…I've
been sensing you all day…

NINA: Is anyone here?

(As he brings her inside:)

ALEX: No.

NINA: *(Looking around:)* Lock the door. Someone might
come in.

ALEX: No one will come in. They're at supper.

NINA: I know your mother's here. Lock the door.

ALEX: It doesn't lock. I'll shove a chair against it. *(He
does.)* Don't worry, no one's coming in.

NINA: *(Looking at him:)* I want to look at you, Alex.
Really look at you.*(Then she can't and looks around.)* It's
so nice here. So warm and comfortable… This used to
be the dining room, didn't it?

ALEX: Yes…

NINA: Have I changed much?

ALEX: …Yes.

NINA: I know.

ALEX: Nina, why wouldn't you let me see you? I know you've been here almost a week. I've been going to the inn every day and they told me you wouldn't let me up.

NINA: Because you hate me.

ALEX: No, I—

NINA: I don't blame you… Every night I dream I see you and you don't recognize me. Let's sit down. *(she sits.)* Let's talk and talk, just like the old days, just like we used to…Alex!… *(She holds his hands, holds back tears)* It's alright. What was I saying?

ALEX: Nina?…

NINA: Yes…I'm fine… Last night I walked out there to see if our stage was still standing…and when I saw it, I just sat and cried, and cried and cried. It's the first time I cried in two years…I felt better… So… You're a writer now! And I'm an actress! Just like we hoped… *(She starts to cry again, wiping away tears.)* We were so happy when we were young, weren't we, Alex?

ALEX: You're still young.

NINA: No, no… Before…remember? I loved you so much, I couldn't keep my hands off you…and we both dreamed of who we'd be… Oh, never mind. I have to go. I have to be up early to take a flight to… *(Laughing through tears)* …fucking Cleveland…can you believe it?

ALEX: Why Cleveland?

NINA: I have a part in a play there. Nothing much…

ALEX: Oh, Nina. I did hate you. Or I told myself I did. I tore up all your letters and your pictures but still…I always knew I loved you…I'll always love you. Nina… Ever since I lost you, my life hasn't made sense. I feel like I'm a hundred years old now, like somehow my youth—my life—got snatched away and disappeared. I see your face everywhere, your beautiful smile. And I know the happiest days of my life are gone. I already lived them.

NINA: Why are you telling me this…?

ALEX: Because I have no one but you. I never had anyone but you. I'm completely alone, and all I care about is being with you. I can't get warm, Nina! Everything I write is somehow half-dead. Nina, stay with me. Please. Or let me come with you.

NINA: Why do you say you still love me? You should kill me…after all I've done to you… Like you shot that seagull, remember? …Except there's no point now. He already did it. Exactly like he said he would. I'm a seagull, a subject for a short story…

(Noises off. Laughter. MARIA *and* PHILIP*)*

NINA: Oh… he's here!? I see… Oh, well… Of course he's here… *(Getting her coat)* Do you know he laughed at me? He laughed at my dreams of becoming an actress. After all that encouragement he gave me to leave here…he fucking laughed at me!? Maybe because he realized I wasn't any good… And maybe I wasn't… You have no idea how horrible it is to be in the middle of a scene and not know what to do with your hands or your voice… I couldn't think or feel anything. Of course, I was pregnant—and I lost the baby—and he wouldn't come home at night, and I knew he was seeing…your mother…but I shouldn't have been thinking about that when I was on stage! It was awful, Alex. It was so awful…I know when you came to see me perform, you were ashamed of me, weren't you? I understand. I was ashamed of myself.

(Hugs her)

ALEX: No, no… Nina—I…

NINA: But it's alright because now, I'm a real
actress. I'm—I'm a good actress. I can't wait to get to
Cleveland. It's a small part, but I already feel myself
getting stronger and more confident every day.
Remember how we used to pretend we were famous
and we'd read all about famous writers and actors…?
Well, I don't care about that anymore. All I want is to
work. Just do my work no matter where, for no matter
how much money. Do the work for the sake of the
work, and knowing that's all I want and that's all that
really matters, makes me…happy…I have a calling;
I have a purpose, and that's more than most people
have… Right…?

ALEX: Yes…that's more than most people have…
(Pause) I wish I had a calling. I'm just adrift…in images
of my own making, and they're no use to me or anyone
else.

NINA: When I get really, really good and I'm really
proud of my work, will you come see me perform?
Promise me you'll do that?

ALEX: …Yes…

NINA: *(She gets light-headed for a moment.)* I haven't
eaten all day.

ALEX: Stay here, I'll get you some supper.

NINA: No…I have to go. …Why did she bring him
here? Don't tell Philip you saw me. Alright?…

ALEX: I don't speak to Philip.

NINA: I still love him, I do, I do, oh, God, I love him
more than I ever did…I'm a subject for a short story…
What was I saying? …Alex! Do you remember how
sweet we were, how sweet our feelings were for each
other? We were so excited about what our lives would
be, and… We had no idea… *(She closes her eyes.)* Let's
see… *(Reciting from the play:)* "Men, lions, eagles, bears,

geese, antelope; tiny creatures invisible to man's eyes—all forms of life—all life has ended and become extinct. No living creature walks the earth. No gull cries on the shores of the sea, no owl hoots from its perch in the wood. The earth is silent. Cold. Empty. The oceans are dead. The bodies of the living have turned to dust. That dust has turned to stone, to water, to clouds. The souls of the living have become one soul. I am that soul. I am man. I am woman. I am beast. I remember all that was—glorious and venal—human and bestial—I am alone. My voice echoes in the void, unheard. Man has destroyed the earth.

(Impulsively, NINA hugs ALEX and runs out the glass doors. He goes to his writing table, stares at his work, then closes his computer. Takes pages he's written, starts to tears them, then takes a stack of pages he's written and throws them into the air. Exhilarated, he exits through the glass doors, leaving the doors open. The wind scatters the papers.)

(After awhile, the others return, BEN first, pushing the door in, then pushing the chair out of the way. Seeing the papers and the open doors, he gets concerned.)

BEN: It's quite an obstacle course, isn't it? Excuse me. *(He exits through the glass doors then starts to run towards the beach.)* Alex!

(Entering last:)

MARIA: What's all this paper? It's a mess in here. What has Alex been up to? Really. He can be so sloppy… *(Pause, as she starts to pick up the papers)*

(A muffled sound of a gun shot comes from behind the stage near the water. MARIA freezes. a look of horror flashes across her face.)

MARIA: What was that?

(MARIA runs out the doors. BEN comes towards her and takes her back into the house.)

MARIA: What was that? I think I heard something.

BEN: No, no. It was nothing… A truck fired on the beach…

MARIA: It reminded me of—

BEN: Of course, of course.

MARIA: Well...

(All work to recover.)

MARIA: Shall we go back to our game? Philip? Whose turn is it…Milly…

(They become engrossed in the game)

MARIA: Oh Nicky darling, what can we possibly do with these terrible letters?

NICHOLAS: I hate this game.

MARIA: *(To* NICHOLAS*)* …This is Alex's favorite game…

(After a pause)

BEN: Philip, can I speak with you…alone ?

*(*PHILIP *looks at* BEN*. From* BEN*'s look he realizes with dawning horror that* ALEX *just shot himself and that he is dead.)*

*(*MARIA *looks up, sees* PHILIP*. Terrified, she turns to* BEN*.)*

MARIA: What?… *(As the horror hits her:)*

(Slow fade to black)

END OF PLAY